Mundell Country

Mundell Country

New Poems by **William Mundell**

THE STEPHEN GREENE PRESS
BRATTLEBORO, VERMONT

To
My Mother and Father
Flora Gould Mundell 1880-1972
Allie Franklin Mundell 1880-1969
Who set no boundaries to MUNDELL COUNTRY

Acknowledgements

Grateful acknowledgement is made to the following publications for permission to reprint poems that originally appeared in their pages: American Forests; Bitterroot, The New York Quarterly, Poet Lore, The Rhode Islander Magazine in The Providence Journal, The Troubadour.

This book has been produced in the United States of America: designed by Bill Schommer, Graphics, composed by Wordgraphics, printed and bound by Griswold Offset Printing. It is published by the Stephen Greene Press, Brattleboro, Vermont 05301.

Library of Congress
Catalog Card Number: 77-20131
Mundell, William D.
I. Title.
PS 3563.U45M8 811'.5'4
International Standard
Book Number: 0-8289-0327-1

77 78 79 80 81 82 87654321

Contents

Sunride

In his steel-cold stable
I waited where his bridle hung
starred with jewels of dew.
He moved to daisies
one by one. As he
lowered his head
to the meadow's full manger
I saddled the sun.

Gold road and dust of cumulus:
we ran the hilltop islands
on the morning's mist.
Slanting we plumed
the high hawk's wings
with sudden fire.

Sparks from his hooves
filled to flood-mark
rivers that streamed like ribbons
in the valley's dark.

Light from his glistening flanks
revealed white mansions
in the towering clouds.
His head was toward the darkened sea.

I leaped to paths where mottled shade
wove on the northern slope
soft carpet made
with moss and lichens.
From that low foliage rose
pale mushroom moons. Wood shone
and onyx glazed the common stone.

The Strangers

By a sudden bed of the shadowed road
they came to the village, strangers aloof
as the scudding clouds. The farms lay misty
with morning haze. The cattle grazed outward
toward their mid-day pastures. The groves
were sleeping like gardens in growing summer.

Perhaps the visitors saw the wild geese
in the swale at the edge of the marsh,
or a cotton-tail leaving the traffic
of the graveled way.

They passed all the little roads
leading back to the higher farms. They passed
the small white church and the burial ground.

Rounding another bend of the road
they were gone. They will not remember
where they heard the loudest bird
of summer, or remember the quiet town
or ever return.

An Absence

I come back to where I have always been.
There is silence in the rooms,
a clutter of things: books,
a beach of gathered stones,
a wall of landscapes, striving plants.

I place a chair at my father's desk,
cross the day on his calendar.
I dust my mother's paintings.
The wind-caught cumuli drift
afresh in their skies;
deer cross in their deeper woods.

Here in the stones: Mexico, Arizona.
I take copper from the Lavender Pit, chrysocolla.
Crossing the Rio Grande
I carry geodes, onyx, scenic agate.
From a sack I draw amethyst,
the roar of the Bay of Fundy.

I open a book, Fifty Poems
and go shelling on Sanibel:
Here is my Lady's Ear and Heart Cockle,
Lion's Paw and Lettered Olive.
Under the asparagus fern
a fawn nuzzles the hand of Saint Francis,
a bird alights in his outstretched palm.

I come back to where I have always been.
A desert lies on the fields of snow.
A sea mounts in the conifers.
The rooms fill with voices.

Mike Of The Gravel Pit

I dig for Him in the gravel pit.
The stones fall down saying His name.
The blood lags in my arms seeking that strength
to raise the cold stones up to light again.

I work my failing muscles here for Him,
watching the agate eyes and quartz for signs.
I know, I know beyond the gold I earn,
I lay up treasure working His hard mines.

I go a narrow way to the open pit,
my senses blunted as the pick I swing.
I find a beauty in the wild, tiered earth,
a pleasure that may be a sensual thing.

I dig for Him in the stony pit.
Whatever my earthly fate, I dig for Him.
I trip, I fall and I crawl up again
toward a stern heaven that may not let me in.

Valley Of Elah

Out of a boisterous army
singled, I move to that honor
of lone victory,
bearing against the delicate morning
a countenance dark as storm,
chill as the ice blue light
from my armour,
my shadow holding the frost
of night.

A shepherd child is sent
to my challenge,
a child, bending to patches
of sunlight and flowers.

Surely this terrible pain
in my forehead, this dizziness,
will pass,
this blur in my sight,
this light on the wings
of a hovering bird,
my sword flashing above me
in the hands of a boy!

The Decision

Dorr knew that if he allowed the loggers
to cut his forest it would be the right thing to do,
though afterward his heart would feel as scarred
as the hill after the work of the crew.

By fall pine limbs would be rust red and tinders,
fewer green needles to shine against the sky,
undergrowth would be caught in the whirlwind of logging,
the spared thin trees looking ready to die.

Snow would cover the waste of the fallen birches,
their limbs spalling before he could gather the wood.
Brush would lie, a barricade to his acres,
blackberries grow up where the timber stood.

He visioned his maple grove piled high on the skidway.
He had thought he never would let the maples go,
or that ever in spring he would stand
at their bleeding stumps knowing
it was the last time their sap would flow.

Speaking For The Seed Potato

After earth's upheaval,
the sun's drying, the sacking,
after the siege of bins,
the cities of cellars,
my eyes grew in the night.
I knew my fellows.

I slept my days remembering
brothers of stone
...like me, my shape, my size,
hardly more mineral than I.
I asked what they might lack:
they knew no eyes!

They knew no force to live
for which I am destroyed each day
(O moons and spinning suns!)
They do not know this tragedy
of birth and death,
of my frail permanence
-being uprooted,
then put back in earth.

Bike Ride

Hop picking at Canajoharie
diminished to a saturday burn
on the fingers. A new ache
worked out of the legs
as the pedals pumped the rhythm
of a heart steadied for a journey.

Gold sand to Stone Arabia
ran easy on the high, thin wheels
then the road, paved with heat
blurred like a mirage
into Broadalbin.

Even now, in sunlight
and wide country, remote ranges
held their intimacy with night.
The mind formed sleek shadows
to shapes neither animal nor human
that faded into rippling water,
into mottled grass.

Sleep in Saratoga – the old home –
the mineral springs. Still all night
a wind-sound stalked the fields
where the trembling light
of dawn must pass.

Noon at Schuylerville,
the Hudson crossed; then shadows leaned
to take the eastward lead.

A thread of sky above evergreens
held the slim trail as night
pressed its leaden wish upon Arlington.

Wilderness ahead, dismounted,
walking uphill, the vacant sawmill,
the Kelley Stand was passed.

Fear came
on the steep road to Stratton.
A presence following
could be felt in the chill air,
closing, closing the safe distance
to the warm body, the pounding heart,
a presence testing its power
to frighten with pressure of unseen eyes
that electrified the pores, bristled the hair.

Whatever moved in the panther woods
found no victim – the timing off,
the crest was gained. Once more
the man, astride his wheel,
shed fear piecemeal at every downhill mile.

Morning painted the Wardsboro hills
in sunrise pastures leading to Newfane.
My father found his father's father well
and found my mother with her grey-green eyes.

Battlefield

I was running again,
breaking ranks in after-school hurry,
turning crosslots
to the home haying field
over bar-way and stream and line-tree hedge
to the harvested hill
where in the blue wind
the gathered hay lay golden
at my feet.

I was among reapers again
wishing to be blessed by the tired hands
and prove the measure
of my helping strength
by the beads on my forehead.

The reapers fled as from an enemy
hurrying their wooden rakes and heavy cart.
Turning, their eyes pierced me
as cleanly as a gleaning tine.
Wounded I ran through the field
stabbing each golden tumble
with my bayonet, hearing only
the dry scream of the grass.

For J.W.A.

Because I saw the sun through tears
pristine, aloof, its warming rays
indifferent to joy or grief
—so I shall tolerate the days.

The moon arose oblique through mist
vapid with cold and neutral light
nor touched the coombs of hill or heart
—so I shall tolerate the night.

I remember laughter, love,
that the great wheel of days winds on,
that man is more than flesh or stone
—so I shall tolerate the dawn.

The Hanging

The knot of his hanging noose was made with seven rings.
One was for love, love, the word for a summer
or any ephemeral thing.

For beauty one of the circling rings was placed,
beauty to whom the knee was eagerly bent.
beauty demanding all.

For deep desire one of the rings was wound,
desire of the covetous eyes, the mind's insatiable thirst.

One of the circling rings was laid for pride
that turned his feet to the hopeless height of dreams,
out of the common streets, the narrow streams.

One of the winding lays was placed for fault;
fault of ignorance, fault of knowing,
fault of going when all was lost,
and sometimes the fault of winning.

One lay of his hanging noose was wound for time,
time that stole youth's step, youth's look,
for subtle time that told no end of time.

One of the winding lays was wound for fear:
fear of the free, the unmarked way,
fear of a contrite heart, a heart that sings.

One ring was wound for fear of his hanging rope.
His hanging knot held well with its seven rings.

The Sugaring Road

We couldn't wait to plow those drifting lanes
that bring the hillside grove of maples back
to us from winter isolation
in snow so deep no creature dared his track.

It seems like shaking hands to touch the bark
of orchard trees we tapped another year.
We open up a circle of old friends;
our roads invite new visitings of deer.

Morning will bear us on its icy rails
while each day thaws until we pass
spring's reddening shoots, protruding rocks,
and mud our runners press from greening grass.

On Hunter's Hill

I know that cloak of wind
the eagle folds about him
when searching he becomes but eyes
that press and chain;

that shield of song
the forest holds,
those arrows of ceased melody
flung from a silent bow;

that hand,
those sunlight fingers
touching darkened woods.

I know the oil of waters,
the stone's wet glaze
that soothes the snail;
the crystal cup
the ledges hold that filters down
to where roots weave their sunless maze.

The Porcupine

A lumbering grey porcupine
gnaws at the tool-shed door,
knowing the seepage of halite,
salt for the winter path,
is the sure medicine-cup
to set his digestion right.

He could be tasting
the bitter gum of a spruce;
but for whom besides he
was this house built on
lookout ledges above a world
of valleys where wind rapids
try the timbers and sweep the stone bare?
For whom was this vestibule made
with sides sharply angled
like a comforting cave?

He was cornered here.
He turned his back to the intruder
and stood for the blow,
lifting his hands
in a gesture like prayer.

What then is a gnawed beam
or a hole to be patched
in the tool-house floor?
The intruder laid down his axe
and opened the door.

The Kittens

Under dry shingles of the rained-on roof,
taunted by the dog-dayed season,
high in attic eaves, farthest from the rising river,
the kittens were born wet on a dusty pallet
and dried by the dry tongue of their mother.
Blind to their darkness, they rested, listening
to the purring sound of distant water.
They were found at last by poking hands.
They clung to the splintery rafters as fingers
closed around them, feeling their softness.
With a cold stone to nuzzle for a mother
they were placed in a burlap bag
and were carried down to the swollen river.
They were flung in the stream at the swiftest bend
crying once in a little voice before they drowned.

An Aging House

Punish me storm
for hoarding the sun's gold
in my shingles,
for storing silver
in my boards.

Pelter me
for empty days,
for too much laughter.
Soothe me with pain,
a broken window.
Let rain in.

Avenge the sun.
Storm ride over me.
Laugh my pride down
with brittle thunder.
When I am low,
grass, leaf, flower
gently cover me.

THREE POEMS: NORWALK HOSPITAL

Requiem For A Fisherman

Rock him, cradle, boat, bed,
back to the sea's escape,
the seascape, the going out
under the gull's cries,
the night-watch in the dim harbor.

Let the uniform whitecaps
be buoyant waves.

Let the mind cast
a net wrought of star-thread,
the eyes haul in
loaves, fishes, riches,
moongold from the sea's trough,
a calm on the waters.

Rock him, cradle, boat, bed,
back to the sea's escape,
the seascape, the going out
under the gulls' cries.

View of Sacco Sound

The harbor invites my gaze.
I walk seaward
along the curving sand
onto the stepping stones
of boats that move
into the mysterious haze.

I am invited to voyage,
to find harbor in that distance.

The nurse pulls the draperies
silently as a far passing train.

Spinal Tap (The Duck Pond)

Pools of darkness fill
where light leaks
from shimmering ripples
that move on the mirror
of the pond.

I float mesmerized
knowing a false peace.

The predator watches
from a center of shadows.
Lost light gathers
in great owl eyes.

Deftly
a talon pierces my spine.

Talk With Will Tobey

I climbed cross-lots above Brown's pasture
to visit with Will Tobey
zigzagging through thick junipers
the rabbits love.
Over one hill, across Brown's brook,
over another wall with strand of rusted wire
lay Tobey's land.

Winds brushed aside the grasses
for my feet, wide as any bed
where deer have lain.
His field was sown
more to goldenrod than grain.
Paths, like spokes, ran everywhere
to meet the forest's rim of trees.
I'd think to ask Will Tobey about these
and speak to him about the drouth of seed.

His meadow was a place where winds
from all ways gathered in
like waves to shore
and bore the hawk so still and steadily
it seemed I felt his gaze.

A hedge of lilac pushed at Tobey's door.
His house revealed a weathered look
I had not noticed there before.
He was about the place somewhere in shadow.
I heard him mending something
in the blacksmith shed.
Old leather swayed upon a wooden pin.
Overhead a squirrel braked his entrance in.

Old Tobey heard my talk about the fallow ground,
the task of one man plowing all alone.
I think he answered me:
"You know the boys are gone for now;
they're almost men. But they'll be coming back.
The farm won't lack," he said, "the farm won't lack."

The sun shot through an opening in the roof
to show the shed was empty,
as though I needed proof, or yet to warn
me not to talk to shadows.
...I half remembered then
that someone said Will Tobey died
the year that I was born.

In Mingling Wood

One day in the mingling wood
a partridge, expecting to be frightened,
found his fright in the sound of my steps.

Drumming alarm, he divided the forest
with the knife of flight.

As soon as the line was struck
a growing difference appeared.
The somber oak, the nervous pine
readied contest for the ground.

Heedless of battle save their own
chase and chatter squirrels came
scattering leaves, blurring the line
in no-man's land.

Both sides drew to their careless game
and the woods returned to a mingling wood.

The Deaf Man Is The Dry Brook

all sound is drained out of him
except pools of memory
that are the mirrors of his songs.

His eyes miss the laughter
of the child-romping water,
the tantrum stream.

The peace of his silence lies
a leaden storm in the flowering sky
where clouds roll for the weather.

He taps the rock with his cane
a ritual for rain
that he may hear again
with his eyes.

Hail Nymphs And Metamorphoses

Hail ambush bugs (insect opossums).
Hail fierce fire ants and antlered flies,
green lacewings, frail and filmy things
with golden eyes, lacewings that hatch
the aphis-lions; hail dragonflies.

This is the age of beetles
judged by the number of their species
when millions, microscopic, literally
can swarm through eyes of needles,
and others, giant walking sticks,
can cut through jungled tropics.

Note Hercules of Africa,
The Pigmies (microlepidoptera),
insect of stagnant water,
the froghopper that controls
his climate in a froth on weeds.
Count aphids and the katydids,
foam castles of cercopids.

The scarab beetles of the Nile
yet hold to that life pattern
that they knew under Pharoah's rule,
while other insects, minor,
still "wheel their droning flights",
and as in 1000 B.C.
crickets still chirp in China.

In what fine drift have men
as riders of the air
invaded space and planet
or on the surface of the swells
moved fair as insect hosts
or sure as water-striders?

In what rare pitch can men preserve
their kind for fifty million years,
like gems in some transparent chamber
as bright as ruby skeletons
of ants in Baltic amber?

–And now, oldest of living insects,
pale, wingless, streamlined creature,
a feature of earth's fauna,
the enduring silverfish devours
print, paste and page,
and poems transient as these hours.

The Ballad Of Dana Hutton

Plow-wracked Dana
with a gall backed horse
and a toe-out stride
plowed a rock strewn course

through his hill-slant fields.
He turned all the sod
to the highway's edge
and he plowed a good rod

of the town's right-of-way.
It was land, land, land
for his corn, corn, corn;
did one care to understand.

Dana was mighty
putting in the seeds,
tall above the kernels,
lord above the weeds.

Dana was a match
for the stalks half grown,
head above the green shoots
he hoed all alone.

Dana grew short
as the corn grew tall
--lost in the field;
no sight of him at all.

Dana grew smaller
as the fall frost came
and turned the meadows brown
and his corn turned the same.

Dana was a little man,
cutting corn stalks down,
making wigwam cities
on the pumpkin ground.

Dana grew taller
as the corn went in;
some to the silo,
some to the bin.

Dana was a tall man
all the winter through.
Forking cows their fodder
he was well-to-do.

Dana was a thin man,
old and slightly bent
when his corn had vanished
all his wealth was spent.

In spring he was a poor man
—and what could he do now
but harness up the old horse
and fasten on the plow.

Transition

A fox is digging by the barn door
trying to enter an empty place.
Why didn't I finish cutting
the unwanted grass?
Why didn't I fight back
the advancing trees.

I would have him understand
if I could, that he is encroaching
upon my land.
He would have it that I recognize
my field has entered into his wood.

Carnival

Riding this Ferris Wheel of days
each passenger can feel his heart's elation
when it is his chair that swings
precariously there at the summit.
He sees things again in the old way.
His eyes have their moment of vision
before he plunges back
to the midway crowd,
the certainties of the day.

Vying for attention in this paper alley
are a dozen fronts to side shows of the mind.
Behind the calendars from the local garages
some watch the dancers; some look at the animals.
Some have placed their money on the wheel of fortune.
The winners hold bright blankets as prizes.
Do you hear the spiel of the barkers?
They would draw you in with fast talk.

Will you challenge the weight-guessers, the age-guessers?
Notice some players have won bright canes and walk
a few quick steps with their old swagger.

See the confidence of those artists
who without benefit of nets perform hourly -
every cough and sneeze an awkward stumble
in their tightrope act?
They fumble and recover. The act is not over
and today is always practice for tomorrow.

In No Still Place

The winds breathe flatteries
about such architecture
as the spider builds.
The sun (early harvester)
hastes toward his vineyard
of morning dew.

Under the springing sod
the water sings
its channel soundings
in the muted earth.

Calm aerialist,
artist of pantomime
above the spreading nets
of worm-laced leaves,
the acrobatic ant receives
the grasses' long applause.

The bee, wide wanderer,
stranger to his own field,
finds all things new.

In this changeless place
the world is changed.
Deeper than furrows where
the plowman ran his share,
the earthworm carves the soil
to his own plan.

Mister Hopkins

Joe, living alone, allowed old Fay
to board the winter months with him.
Fay, more of a tramp
than a neighbor or friend to anyone,
lived, summers, in deserted houses
on back-road farms. They were his wealth
after their worth was gone.
Fay watched them slowly crumble
into their cellars.
He would grumble then and move his belongings
to another shelter with a better roof.

Fay's summers were not spent in idleness.
He was custodian of wild berry patches,
the gunny sack inspector of abandoned orchards.
Sometimes he was a scarecrow
watching in the green rows of others' gardens.
Springtimes he would tap a near maple
and boil the sap in his teakettle.
There would be syrup enough for one breakfast.

Fay was good company for Joe;
useful in steadying one end of a crosscut saw
when Joe was ready to cut firewood for a chilly night.

Fay was willing to earn his keep.
He liked Joe's table:
the potatoes, salt pork and milk gravy.
Whenever Joe left to go to the store
Fay hurried to test the cider in the cellar,
gather any fresh eggs he could find
to cook and eat before Joe returned.
If he knew which hen was laying
he would hide her in a back shed
to be sure of her eggs for himself.

Whenever someone stopped to talk
Fay always smiled and never once forgot
to add the "Mister" to the person's name.
Maybe because he was never called
anything but "Fay" himself.
It didn't matter that in an earlier day
he claimed for himself a modest fame.
His picture had been printed on a postcard
that sold in the local store.
It showed a group of hunters posed about a panther.
Fay was kneeling at the dead animal's tail.

Some said Fay lacked the will for honest work,
that with comfort grew less robust than he knew.
With all his luck he didn't last the winter through.
The town authorities looked up his next of kin.
Two of Fay's rich brothers came in limousines.
They arranged a proper and expensive funeral for him.

The Fun Of Hollerin'

Seldom was there more excitement
in Addie's kitchen than that caused
by a burnt pie. Even that could be pleasant,
when it sent a Greening-apple odor
through all the rooms, whetting
appetites for the coming meal.

Now their new neighbor stood at her door
with mud to his knees.
Addie knew he needed her Henry
and the horses to pull his car
out of the quagmire the road became
every time it rained.

Henry was mowing in the field,
that rolling region you could see
from the hayloft door.
They would wave to him from there.
They saw him – the horses first –
ears, heads, hames, then Henry
and the loud machine came over the hill.
– but he was watching the cutter-bar,
the grass snapping to attention
then falling backward in the swath.

He squared his corner, headed round
and disappeared over the knoll again.
Next time around Addie waved her apron
and shouted a little louder.
They had to laugh being so far
from his attention.
Addie was enjoying the challenge.
She kept right on shouting
until the neighbor despaired.
"No, he ain't going to hear us from here,"
she said. "But we did have the fun of hollerin'!"

The Visit

It was a carefree walk
over the shadowed lawn,
past the dark of the garden spot
and on—all the way under
the butternut tree
to the road.
He saw me,
Old Moore, the butcher.
He wanted to talk.
"Folks know you're here?"
Glancing back to his shed
where long knives shone in a rack
catching the morning light,
I could not speak.
The sawdust floor was red.

He was pleased I had come.
He smiled for some secret wish fulfilled
to be visited by a child.

"Stay a minute," he said.
He entered his lonely house
and brought me honey and bread.
I took it:
a saucer with golden band
and honey cut from the comb
with the skill of a butcher's hand.

For a moment I held my ground.
I eyed him man to man.
Blood drained from my outstretched arm,
the saucer crashed,
and I ran!

The Box

We drove out to visit Grandpa Evans.
We heard that he wasn't feeling well;
but there he was, his beard washed white,
his clothes bathed in a shaft of light
that spotted him through his dooryard tree.

He was building a box, nailing a box,
shaving a box as skillfully
as thin, frail hands of an old man could,
of wide pine boards new from the mill.
We wondered why, for the weathered house
needed those boards about its sill.

We touched it with respect and stared.
He offered us an apology
that the broad board hinged for a proper lid
showed several knots and a slender crack.
"Things I can fix," he said, "you'll see;
and anyway if I should live
I'm planning on painting
the whole thing black."

The Offering

I, lord of the feast,
who give or withhold
meat or milk
for the pale tongue's cupping
give not enough.

The warm bird
choosing in spring fields
those hairs of grass
for the egg's home
gives all;

becomes in that instant
a leaf severed
by the saber of wind,
mist seized by sunlight,
the night pinned by lightning.

Lord of the feast,
I receive an offering,
a wing placed at my door:
Isaac upon the altar.

Lottie Wonders

An old woman poking
a cane among her ruins
uncovers only a frost,
a surface hiding the truth
of wood decayed, of brick
that is rubble. The earth lies blurred
under a glass of forgetfulness.

Almost she is tripped
by the leash of the wind.
Her hands grope out...
she has the old hound by the head.
"Steady there! Steady!"
...and she is obeyed.

Was life dancing the moon down,
strong hands clasped, and song trailing
into the long goodnight?
Was it like that past remembering,
past what the heart now feels
—except that then the old dog of the wind
was a pup at her heels?

Petunia The Dachshund's World

I swim on my back
across seafoam carpet,
the nylon pebbles combing
my seal-black hair.
I know this beach,
the safety of this shore,
my lifeguard master.

On the terrace at Cooper Hill
a tide of air comes
scented with mysteries.
In that moment
when the wind's knell
drowns the clang
of my tinker bell
I dive unnoticed
out of sunlight
into evergreen depth
to face the tooth and claw
of darkness.

I sharpen my teeth
on a wasting bone
turned chalk by winter.

My icy nose
shivers the stone
of a snail's cold shell.
I leave my scent
where chipmunks run.
I startled one
who dropped his supper
of seeds and fled.

Beside the mound
of a woodchuck burrow
the sun's eye stares
from a snakeskin scale.
I pin it twice
with a snap of jaw;
I shake it down
to its silver tail
and rounding home,
I leave it there
for the moon to see!

An Offer

Ray Annis wouldn't sell his rough two acres
that jabbed into Phil Wootton's wood lot like an arrow,
particularly to one like Wootton who could buy
any land that touched his outstretched borders.

Phil, trying to wear down Ray's stubbornness,
courted his friendship over several seasons,
always asking questions Ray could answer:
how his outmoded chain saw might be working,
or if he needed money for his taxes.

One day he found Ray Annis where he boarded
when he was working for his neighbor
or when Taft brook was running high,
there being no bridge crossing to his cabin.

Ray was sunning on warm kitchen steps
and Phil commenced a careful conversation
that, he hoped, in time
might wind around to business.

Just as he heard Phil Wootton raise his offer
of what he'd give to own the Annis acres,
Ray excused himself by saying, "Just a minute,"
and hurried off somewhere inside the house.

Phil waited on the steps for twenty minutes,
then thirty. He was worried. He sought the lady
of the house and asked if Ray was having trouble
in deciding. She checked his room and soon returned.
"You'll have to wait a bit," she said,
"to get your answer.
I guess that one could say he's sleeping on it."

Nero At Wind Rapids

A glacial vapor frets my parapet
cool with the pungent scent of pine;
below the hills flame in October light
–and I am fiddling while the autumn burns.

Show me where his maple columns stood
in fiery arches; did he fall there
amid the ruins of the ashen trees;
and did he die with rhymes upon his tongue?

What phoenix rises in the azúre smoke
lifting the candle flickerings of his verse?
Whose sure hand translates him now
in cloud white sentences across the sky?

Wing Clipping

Spring came and all that blazing green
inside the hen yard could be seen
by penned-in chickens that had spent
a winter of imprisonment.
Released, their yard was paradise,
a garden set before their eyes,
enticing each bird of the flock
to pick at every leaf and stalk
until, too soon, the ground was bare
and dust and dust holes everywhere
looked like the craters of the moon.

Always there's one bird that is wise
enough to dream of broader skies,
one bird that will always try
to act like spring's first butterfly.
We lost a hen or two that way.
I was appointed there and then,
before the whole flock disappeared,
to clip one wing of every hen.
–just the feather tips, so when
they tried to fly they'd spiral wide
and land back on the penned-in side.

I guess the sound of scissors made
them apprehensive for they laid
a cloud of dust across the yard.
Hens went flying everywhere;
some close to ground, some high in air.
They formed a circle out of reach,
yet now and then above the dust
I saw bright feathers shine that must
have been the sight that Custer saw.
I felt no arrows but a claw
drew blood, and wounded, I found
myself like Custer on unconquered ground.

New Shoes

It was his shoes, he thought,
which were never clean of loam,
that above them no one could guess
earth was his pavement at home.

He bought the best new shoes
for the city looked at his feet,
but his heels seemed never to click
in tune with the shining street.

He walked as a man would walk
whose shoes were a badge and shield.
He strode down the furrowed street—a youth
who at home would be plowing a field.

Bargain

At times the villagers envied old Clem.
He borrowed things from everyone around
and managed to make out a better fare
than most of those he borrowed from had found.

He'd borrow maybe half a cup of sugar,
a cake of soap, but never quite enough
that anyone would ask it be returned
or bother to remember all the stuff.

"Good neighbors are good lenders," he would say.
We all admired the practiced art he used
but never knew his shrewdness until one day
he came when Pa was cutting down a butchered critter.

Pa cornered him and said, "Now Clem,
I'll give you a front quarter free and clear
if you won't borrow from me for a year."
He hadn't reckoned all the worth Clem put
upon the right to borrow for that while.

Pa said, "Of course you'll miss some little things,
but you wouldn't pass a deal like that up would you?"
Clem thought, then put his answer squarely,
"Now you couldn't make that a hind quarter, could you?"

Brook Frozen Over

This dawn you cannot hear
the brook's low song.
Ice has closed a door;
the still hours are long.

Listen, listen to catch
some note and rejoice;
buried deep in the cold
is the warmth of a voice.

Do not trust ears
that knew summer to tell
if the green sounds are gone.
They have learned them too well.

Listen! The wind
would be neighbor now
with a rustle of frozen limbs,
the crack of a bough.

The Proof

It is said if you go
by Memorial Height
on an all-out night
of wind and snow
when time draws near
the approximate hour
that the old numb year
stumbles back to its zero,
when jaws of the cold
grip the earth like a vise,

it is said, on such nights,
out of cracks in the ice,
out of mounds on the ground,
out of hollows of trees,
there gathers a force
so strong that it can
for a rather short time
derange the mind
of any who pass.

A man about town
forcefully spoke
of the rumors as false,
that the whole affair
was a stupendous joke
and purposely put
the sayings to test.

So eager he was
to prove them a jest
that he ran to the Height
hardly dressed for the cold.

The way that he laughed
was a fright in itself.
Then he lay down
on a visible mound
to prove, so he said,
just once and for all,
that nothing strange
came up from the ground.

Further to discount
the sayings and please
his own whim for detail
he climbed several trees
that were hollow.
Though he was too large
to get inside of these
he managed to squeeze
his head into one.

To further his word
that nothing absurd
could affect a staid mind
in that neck of the wood,
to show that his limbs,
at that portentous hour
were as strong, as controlled
as any strong man's,

he lighted his pipe
which he put in his mouth
quite bottom side up,
then made everything right,
as one understands,
when he kicked up his heels,
and walked straight away
from that talked-about place
on the palms of his hands.

Spring: Colonial Hilton

Touch me that I may see
magic casements
opening to green seas
of carpet lawn, fields
leading to that blue pool
beneath the pleasure dome,

home to lovers burning back the gloom
of winter drought with captive sun
filtering again through veins
of silver rivers to their source
lighting winter woods
with diamond flame
in every lamp of ice.

Hold me that I may know
radiance of the south
loosening roots to all the thrust
of spring. Warm me–a winter thing–
that I believe again
the force of patient seed,
the close entwining of the vine.

Harvest Magic (Sudden Rain)

Magic hangs in pistoned sleeves
of these machines.
Red and yellow blossoms flash
to scarves of varied greens.

Apparatus plays
its illusive act.
The patter, the keen knives
distract us from the fact

that change moves in the grass.
The stalks stand straight and tall
until still jousting with the wind
they pitch and fall.

Bales and baler's knots outdo
rope trick and acrobat;
rakes at borderland lift out
the rabbit from the hat.

Suspect the storm's half-light,
mirage of mirror steel,
suspect the sleight of hand,
the illusion of the wheel.

Rain beats its quick applause.
The hay piled dry
beneath the scaffold proves
the hand is quicker than the sky.

Unwritten Poem

Chips are scattered like words
I would gather to a poem
for the axe shines in my hands,
wet with the tree's wasting sap.
Something is dying in the world.

I would render stone;
gather the ore to fire
for now afield
the sun pours gold
to flowers.

I would recall lightning,
the mind's flash,
for out of empty sky
in a splash of light
swallows dive.

The poem flares
on the kindled hills.
It is traced indelibly
on the invisible air.

Sphinx

Her golden haunches rise
sphinx-like out of the desert
of the mouse's fear. Her eyes
gaze like the moon that draws
the helpless tides; her calm
is like a lull in threatening skies.

I know the beggar-mouse within her gate,
the dust of empty attics on his feet,
who from his desert regions sees her plate
a towering pyramid, a Pharaoh's store
where treasure lures him and decrees his fate.

What hungering captive could foreknow
her silken form sheathes twenty ivory spears,
her feline craft withholds the killing blow,
and that the lasting hurt
is being captured, toyed with,
and let go?

Unused Scaffold

Who shall clean this scaffold of its hay
risking broad bayonets of the sun
that slant through fiery fissures in the boards
and hold in golden bars the darkened bay?

Who shall sweep this scaffold's dust away,
destroy the laboring spiders' silver wheels,
unhinge the lofting strands the ants must cross
or stomp the hidden tunnels where mice play?

Thin breezes brush the tine-worn planks today
testing the brittle grass, sifting the seed.
A broken straw, a handful of sunlit chaff
fall, like meteors, from slow decay.

Vignette

All her years she fought the dust
until on her coffin it lay with rust.
Her closest intimate at the end
she clasped it to her as a friend.

The Stricken One

He shuffles after shock
one arm a dangling rope
within a sleeve
fingers fisted
like a fraying knot.

With one good hand and stick
he labors past his resting dog
–one foot, one foot–
toward that vague plot
he knows must yield
more happiness than yesterday.

His equal brother
helps him light his pipe.
The sunshine warms him
through his weathered coat;
rare contentment dulls his eyes
as all the insults of the years
burn in forgetfulness.

His smile drivels.
He shouts and scares the dog
and all his muscles twitch in glee,
a prank remembered
of a boy's forbidden play.

The Chopper

Hands fisted to the axe's helve, he
cuts the season back with cadenced blows
unto the secret heartwood of the tree.

He drives his wedges at the trunk's wide girth
until the great tree shuddering in the sky
vaults downward toward the canyon of its birth.

The saw waits soundlessly, the axe lies still.
Silence, like a stunned thing, endures.
–Then one loud crash releases all the hill.

A Distance Builds

One leaf goes
in such quietness
the heart catches
knowing
the subtleties of fall.

In this room
winter's closing drifts
are in your eyes.
A distance builds.
I can not reach
the nearness to your chair.

I call, I call.

—and neither of us ever
can come home again.

Until The Last Earth

What man has made
I do not marvel to see moved
whether by itself, by man
or by the design of nature,
for man is little
and his monsters are small.

But to see a star fall is like
the sun did not rise
and the darkness of sky
is a loss to heaven.

The Bear

Fear was a black bear in the night
only the watch-eyed horse could see
there on the dug-way road
where mountain ledges pressed
the white water stream.

The horse, on one knee,
tried to crawl under the wagon shafts.
My mother, whip in hand,
commanded the horse to stand,
cried "Children, keep close!,"
coached us how to scream.
Whatever was there fled
and we were free.

There is something vague
and dark on the road ahead.
My car knows no fear
as slowly we close
the distance between the bear and me.

I see that narrow road,
the ledges, the tameless stream.
Each mile I become less sure
that I'll have the will,
the saving grace, to scream.

Ice Fern

In darkness, stars of ice,
hinting of form, of branches,
shapes in the half-light of marshes
of the first sea-born continents.

The first draft of tropical islands
evolves in the pattern of fern.
Fronds out of Devonian rock,
our first vegetation,
form in frozen gardens,
still rise in woodlands,

wings singing in light,
rhythmic and dancing,
the pattern of flight,
the first geometry,
the first poetry.

Farmer Morse

He borrowed silence from the silver cold
that froze the pliant stream and hushed
its voice, leaving the stare of ice.

He borrowed patience from the season's pose
that all was well, though roots ached in the ground
and earth's crust knew the nervous swell of spring.

From harvesting he learned a miser's thrift.
to hoard remembrances against lone days
and hungering that could be his.

His faith was as the sower's in the seed,
that out of darkness something moves to light,
that summer nurtures both the flower and the weed.

Miranda (Elegy for a Young Black Cat)

I shall see always
the semicircle of her
curving backward, a black velvet
crescent thin as a new moon,
her eyes probing the wonders
of this world: the darkness
under the huge terrace,
the mysteries that come alive
in the secret chambers of the night,
the loneness of the threatening forest.

Out of the light, out of the dark
she flowed like a leaf upon water,
a leaf in the wind
touching the earth lightly.
She came from the centuries
to teach us the beauty of wildness,
to tolerate our fondling.

She could not judge the monsters
of our making—the murderous cars.
She saw the meteors,
the growing flames,
the darkness, the darkness

—and two small lights went out.

Eligible

Some ladies of the Ladies Aid
at times will chance small gossip
when the quilts are made.
They were sighing, how
Professor Harmon's wife had died
and, now, of his availability
for marriage —and none of them was free
except Betsy. They challenged her.
"You're halfway young,
you're strong, you drive a car,
you own ten acres on the River Road.
Except at moulting time your hens are far
the best white leghorns in the valley.
You could get your teeth repaired
and maybe, by way of introduction,
we could invite Professor Harmon
and the minister to tea.
You're eligible, now ain't you, Betsy?"
they asked again. Betsy was fair.
She recognized her singleness
and answered honestly. "Well, the way
you make it out, I s'pose I be."

Gem Stone

The stone earth,
its white curl of cumulus
a halo flawing its opal blue,
answers the first prayer:
soil, air, sun, water.

Cliffs of the planets...nothing,
mirrors of dust.

I have seen heaven...earth:
springs singing forth rivers,
wells yielding the ore of rain,
the ground lending, giving.

Slug under the rock,
our table is set before us.

The Swamp

The seeds of legends flourish in its quicksand soil
haunted by half-things. A thousand leering
eyes of double-creatures blink and green amphibians

swim in brackish ooze where fog-forms conjure shapes that
walk will-o'-the wisp over vaporous bogs,
and winding weeds and winter's straws tangled with limbs
make witches' brooms. Yet here some strange awakening thing
places rare lady's slippers at the feet of spring.

On Brown's Pasture Road

Slowly the grass erases
the sentence of his paths
for the earth keeps those whisperings
his shoes made
in grooves more certain now
than memory.

They tell he went a clover way to bring
the lingering cows. They show
the place he stood
to swing the pasture gate. They show
the one divergent route
he sometimes took to view the valley
from a look-out ledge.

One path runs sidelong
to the garden's edge
that could have run less windingly.
It tells of one who took the time
to check the growing corn,
or needed time, perhaps
to contemplate whether
to hoe the dew-wet garden
or to let it wait.

At headland green
along the haying road
a steep path tumbles
to a ring of fern. One knows
the hay loads pulled up briefly there...
the stomping horses
rested in that cooler air
while all the hay-hands
drank from the cool spring.

He who walked here
unmindful of his paths
leaves marks carved deeply
in these acres yet.

The sun burns at the grassroots
where he trod.
And at deserted roads
run rain and rivulet.

Sam: A Dedication

Sam was nobody's dog,
everyone's friend.
Was, was, was,
that is the hurting word
that flings him just there
beyond ever coming down
the road again;
that brings his pleading whine
out of the gunning thunder,
shapes him bull strong
in every snow,
draws him bronze
in whirling leaves,
mirrors in rain pools
his gentle eyes
Sam was nobody's dog.
He belonged to the neighborhood.
"There was no place for him,"
said one who had the say.
"I had him put away."

Of One Who Left

This was his village
at the bend of the stream
where the halo of fog
hides in sheltering willows,
where cattle drink slowly
from images in the shining water,
where the line of the road
is dark with stone fences
and the street is pierced in fierce
judgment by the shadow of the steeple.

The houses are gathered as though to answer
in one voice the shout of the morning
and to stand together
against the uncertain night.
Vines of smoke grow out of the chimneys
into the arbor of the sky.

-But of the people of his village;
we can not know of the fire of their hearts,
only the dispassioned swing of the scythe,
the inevitable stride into the seasons.
They do not say if he lost patience,
or in what manner of weeping they let him go.